**Peace Seeker Workbook**
**©2011**
**Peace of Mind Training Institute**

All rights reserved.

ISBN-13: 978-0615472874
ISBN-10: 0615472877

Peace of Mind Training Institute Publishing

No part of this book may be used or reproduced in any manner whatsoever without written permission of Matthew C. Cox, except in the case of brief quotations embodied in critical articles and review.

For information contact:

Peace of Mind Training Institute
21 Pine Ridge Road
Sandia Park, NM 87047
Info@peaceofmindtraininginstitute.com

This workbook belongs to

_____

## A note from Matthew C. Cox

The Peace Seeker Workbook is designed to be a central location for your journey to Peace of Mind. Therefore, it serves two purposes. It is the place for you to answer the Conspiracy Questions located at the end of each chapter in *Living the Southwest Lifestyle; How to Have and Maintain Peace of Mind*. In addition, it is the notebook for the Peace of Mind Seminar presented by The Peace of Mind Training Institute.

Since the journey to Peace of Mind is an internal journey, based on your perspective of the world, it doesn't matter whether you read *Living the Southwest Lifestyle* first or participate in the Peace of Mind Seminar first. The material will lead you to look within and you will receive additional Peace of Mind insight each time you go through it, no matter what order you choose.

## Table of Contents

How to Have and Maintain Peace of Mind ............................................................. 1

Personal Peace of Mind ................................................................................. 19

Relationship Peace of Mind ........................................................................... 30

Financial Peace of Mind ................................................................................. 42

What is the Next Step on My Journey to Peace of Mind? .................................. 59

# How to Have and Maintain Peace of Mind

# Introduction

## An Introduction to Universal Laws

Most belief systems contain _____.

They are _____.

An example of an inconsistency in a belief system is

"Our God of love rules by fear."

Universal Laws cannot be _____.

They are _____.

## The Four Traits of Peace of Mind

1. _____

⊡ What are the inconsistencies in my belief system?

_____
_____
_____
_____

2._____

▣ What sins do I struggle with?

_____

_____

_____

3. _____

▣ What do I feel the need to fight against?

_____

_____

_____

4._____

▣ What do I lack?

_____

_____

_____

_____

## The Three Laws of Peace of Mind

The Law of Miracles - _____

_____

The Law of Attraction - _____

_____

_____

The Law of Abundance - _____

_____

_____

# The Law of Miracles

## Chapter 1

**Conspiracy for Me!**

Through this book, you will learn that Peace of Mind is part of a Conspiracy. You may find the term "Conspiracy" a bit spooky unless you understand the conspiracy is in your favor (and mine).

You will discover that life is a "Conspiracy for Me." You will smile when you see that not only do all things work together for good, all things work together by design for your benefit (and mine and everyone's!)

## Chapter 2

**The Law of Miracles -** Miracles occur naturally as expressions of love.

A miracle is _____

_____

Magic is _____

_____

"Supernatural" events happen outside our _____

Magic operates at the _____

Miracles operate at the _____ levels.

**The Three Elements of The Law of Miracles**

1. Understand Desire
2. Use Thoughts, Words, Actions and Habits to Receive your Desire
3. Know You Always Do Your Best

### 🌀 Conspiracy Question

To help you identify the Universe's Conspiracy for you, most Chapters have a Conspiracy Question to answer. Each question is indicated by a 🌀 (*a labyrinth to remind you to go inside yourself to seek the answer*)

The best way to get the most out of each Conspiracy Question is to write the answer. Use the space provided or a notebook.

# Chapter 3

**ELEMENT ONE – Understand Desire**

Desire means "_____."

All Desires are _____.

A Desire comes from your _____.

It is _____. It is _____.

A want comes from your _____.

It is _____. It is _____.

🌀 What is my Desire?

_____
_____
_____

# Chapter 4

**ELEMENT TWO – Use Thoughts, Words, Actions, and Habits to Receive My Desire**

Receiving my Desire is _____!

I program my subconscious through my _____,

_____, and _____ to create my _____.

This process is _____.

🌀 What changes can I make to integrate my Thoughts, Words, and Actions so I can receive my Desire?

_____
_____
_____
_____

# Chapter 5

**ELEMENT THREE: Know You Always Do Your Best**

🌀 What do I feel guilty about today?

_____
_____
_____

🌀 Whom do I blame for my failures, pains, and discomfort?

_____
_____
_____

🔲 What fears do I have?

_____

_____

_____

_____

I always do my _____.

Everyone else always does his or her _____.

There are no _____.

No mistakes means no _____.

No sin means no _____.

Without guilt, we don't need to _____.

We don't have _____ of punishment.

This produces Miracles because I learn how to _____.

**Remember:** A Miracle is a supernatural shortcut through time and space that happens because of love.

In scientific terms, this is a _____.

_____ causes the leap.

# The Law of Attraction

**The Law of Attraction -** Attraction happens automatically through the principle of sympathetic vibration.

**The Three Elements of The Law of Attraction**

1. My Emotional Intensity Is More Important Than the Emotion
2. My Perspective Determines What I See
3. I Always Get What I Desire

## Chapter 7

▣ When was the last time I felt what someone else felt?

_____

_____

_____

_____

## Chapter 8

**ELEMENT ONE: Emotional Intensity Is More Important Than The Emotion**

All emotions contain _____.

Energy consists of _____.

Objects vibrating at similar frequencies attract through
_____.

▣ What causes me to feel emotional?

_____

_____

_____

_____

🔳 What three emotions do I feel the most often?

_____

_____

_____

## Chapter 9

Another term for sympathetic vibration is _____.

I create energy when I focus on the things I _____.

I create energy when I focus on the things I _____.

Either way, I create energy that _____.

What I focus on _____.

🔳 What do I feel the need to fight against?

_____

_____

_____

_____

_____

# Chapter 10

### ELEMENT TWO: My Perspective Determines What I See

The past determines my _____.

My filter determines my _____.

My perspective is my _____.

When I change my _____, I change my _____.

There are two possible perspectives: _____ or _____.

▣ Do I primarily see life in terms of duality or unity?
_____

▣ Why?
_____
_____
_____

# Chapter 11

### ELEMENT THREE: I Always Get What I Desire

Before birth, God programmed my spirit with my _____.

During childhood, society programs my body/ego to
_____.

This produces a perspective of _____.

A perspective of duality causes _____.

However, I think conflict is caused by _____.

This quote changed Matt's perspective from duality to unity.

> *"It may not seem like luck. It is not. The truth is that life is conspiring in your favor. It may not look that way at the time. However, everything that happens brings you closer to that which you Desire."*

Change is _____.

Conflict is caused by a perspective of _____.

Conflict ends when I change my perspective to _____.

When my perspective is unity, everything leads to my _____.

### It's a Conspiracy for ME!

▣ What does "Life is a Conspiracy for Me" mean to me?

_____
_____
_____

## Chapter 12

**What is Unity?**

Unity is _____!

I see others as _____.

I completely _____.

God/the Universe is orchestrating events to _____;

even the things that, at first appearance, seem to _____.

It means I love all through the practice of _____.

It means I can be completely _____.

It means everything in my life moves me toward my _____.

- Whom do I trust the least?

  _____
  _____
  _____

- What benefit do I receive from my relationship with this person?

  _____
  _____
  _____

- Can I love this person?

  _____

- How can I demonstrate love to this person?

  _____
  _____
  _____
  _____

- What current situation harms me most?

  _____
  _____
  _____

▣ What benefit do I receive from this situation?

_____

_____

_____

# The Law of Abundance

**The Law of Abundance** – Everything reproduces through multiplication over time to produce resources sufficient for all Desires.

**The Three Elements of The Law of Abundance**

1. Abundance is a Normal Act of Nature
2. Lack is Always Temporary
3. Gratefulness Accelerates the Law of Abundance

## Chapter 13

- Do I believe in lack or abundance? _____

- Why?

_____
_____
_____

## Chapter 14

**ELEMENT ONE: Abundance is a Normal Act of Nature**

Nature's design is reproduction through _____.

- What evidence of reproduction through multiplication do I see?

_____
_____
_____
_____
_____
_____

# Chapter 15

**ELEMENT TWO: Lack is Always Temporary**

The only cause of lack is _____.

Preparation for abundance is _____.

An example of preparation for abundance is the _____.

If I see lack as anything else, I have a perspective of _____.

▣ What do I lack?

_____
_____
_____
_____
_____
_____


# Chapter 16

A perspective of duality cause _____, _____, and _____.

Fear, guilt, and blame sometimes feel like _____.

The evidence of fear, guilt, and blame is love with _____.

Resistance creates _____.

Resistance causes us to see lack where there is _____.

🔳 What am I resistant to in my life today?

_____

_____

_____

_____

_____

_____

# Chapter 17

**ELEMENT THREE: Gratefulness and The Law of Abundance**

Gratefulness removes all _____.

The best way to express gratefulness is through _____.

I respond in one of three ways when I receive something.

1. _____
2. _____
3. _____

When I share, I _____.
When I keep, I _____.

When I keep, I _____.

When I reject, I _____

_____.

When I reject, I _____.

What I resist _____.

When I share, I remove _____.

When I share, I fulfill my _____.

🔲 What clutters my life?

_____
_____
_____
_____
_____

## Chapter 18

🔲 How can I immediately demonstrate gratefulness through an act of generosity?

_____
_____
_____
_____
_____
_____
_____
_____

🔲 What can I share today?

_____
_____
_____
_____
_____
_____
_____
_____
_____

# Personal Peace of Mind

## Chapter 20

**The Law of Miracles -** _____
_____

A Miracle is a _____
_____.

The Law of Miracles is the _____

because it works by _____.

I experience Personal Peace of Mind when I identify my

_____ or _____

and recognize there is a Conspiracy for Me to _____.

🔲 Would I consider a supernatural message containing "bad news" to be a Miracle?

_____

# Chapter 21

## The Three Elements of The Law of Miracles

1. Understand Desire
2. Use Thoughts, Words, Actions and Habits to Receive my Desires
3. Know I Always Do My Best

Desire means "_____."

All Desires are _____.

A Desire comes from my _____.

It is _____. It is _____.

A want comes from my _____.

It is _____. It is _____.

1. _____ or _____
2. _____ or _____

🔲 What is my Desire or Life Purpose?

_____
_____
_____
_____
_____
_____
_____
_____

## Chapter 22

I may not trust my ability to hear Divine Guidance directly so I may use an _____.

▣ Who or what are my Intermediaries?

_____
_____

## Chapter 23

The supernatural beings that speak to me are _____.

If I am not comfortable talking to supernatural beings, I may use _____.

▣ What are my mini Desires? What do I like?

_____
_____
_____

▣ What do I like for my Relationships?

_____
_____
_____

*Personal Peace of Mind*

◘ What do I like for my Physical Build and Health?

_____
_____
_____

◘ What do I like for my Money?

_____
_____

◘ What do I like for my Career?

_____
_____
_____

◘ What do I like for my Recreation?

_____
_____

◘ What do I like for my Personal Skills?

_____
_____
_____

◘ What do I like for my Contribution or Legacy?

_____
_____
_____
_____

# Chapter 24

▣ What current habits do I have that keep me from fulfilling my Desire?

_____
_____
_____
_____
_____
_____
_____
_____
_____

# Chapter 25

**ELEMENT TWO – Use Thoughts, Words, Actions, and Habits to Receive My Desires**

Magic is _____
_____.

Supernatural events happen outside our _____.

Events that appear magical are really evidence of The Law of
_____.

The Law of Attraction operates at the _____.

It is _____ and _____.

Miracles operate at the molecular and _____ levels.

Fulfilling my Life Purpose and receiving my Desire is _____.

I program my subconscious through my _____,

_____, and _____ to create my _____.

This process is _____.

I learn to succeed by creating a _____.

Words and thoughts are _____.

◩ Divide my life into three equal periods and list successes in each.

Period One – Age _____

Success 1: _____

Success 2: _____

Success 3: _____

Period Two – Age _____

Success 1: _____

Success 2: _____

Success 3: _____

Period Three – Age _____

Success 1: _____

Success 2: _____

Success 3: _____

# Chapter 26

🔲 Choose a habit you identified in Chapter 24. Write an affirmation to overcome that habit.

_____
_____
_____
_____
_____
_____
_____

# Chapter 27

🔲 What health problems do I experience when I face outside difficulties or conflicts?

_____
_____
_____
_____
_____
_____
_____

# Chapter 28

**ELEMENT THREE – Know I Always Do My Best**

_____, _____ and _____ resist Desire.

▣ What do I feel guilty about today?

_____
_____
_____
_____
_____
_____

▣ Whom do I blame for my failures, pains, and discomfort?

_____
_____
_____

▣ What fears do I have?

_____
_____
_____
_____

## Chapter 29

🔲 When was the last time I morally judged my actions or someone else's?

_____
_____
_____


## Chapter 30

🔲 What Miracle have I experienced in my life?

_____
_____
_____


## Chapter 31

I always do my _____.

Everyone else always does his or her _____.

There are no _____.

Everything I perceive as a mistake is part of the
_____

No mistakes means no _____.

No sin means no _____.

Without guilt, I don't need to _____.

I don't have _____ of punishment.

No sin and no guilt remove the need for _____.

This produces Miracles because I learn how to _____.

I demonstrate love when I am _____.

In scientific terms, this is a _____.

_____ causes the leap.

🔲 What supernatural events have I experienced?

_____
_____
_____
_____
_____
_____
_____
_____
_____
_____
_____
_____
_____
_____

🔲 How have I received guidance from virtual mentors?

_____
_____
_____
_____

_____

_____

I experience Personal Peace of Mind when:

I understand my _____.

I understand all Desires come from _____.

I fulfill those Desires through using the Law of Attraction.

I realize everyone does his or her _____.

    I _____ all.

    I _____ all.

I experience _____.

It is a _____.

# Relationship Peace of Mind

## Chapter 34

▣ What do I feel the need to fight against?

_____
_____
_____

## Chapter 35

The Law of Attraction – _____
_____

**The Three Elements of The Law of Attraction**

1. My Emotional Intensity Is More Important Than The Emotion
2. My Perspective Determines What I See
3. I Always Get What I Desire

▣ What causes me to feel emotional?

_____
_____
_____
_____

# Chapter 36

**ELEMENT ONE: Emotional Intensity Is More Important Than The Emotion**

All emotions contain _____.

Energy consists of _____.

▣ What three emotions do I feel the most often?

_____
_____
_____

# Chapter 37

▣ What three emotions do I feel most intensely?

_____
_____
_____
_____
_____

# Chapter 38

Objects vibrating at similar frequencies attract through
_____

Another term for sympathetic vibration is _____.

I create energy when I focus on the things I _____.

I create energy when I focus on the things I _____.

Either way, I create energy that _____.

What I focus on _____.

🔲 Has there ever been a time in my life when I attempted something and received the exact opposite? Write about that time.

_____
_____
_____
_____
_____
_____
_____

## Chapter 39

🔲 What do I feel the need to defend myself against?

_____
_____
_____
_____
_____

## Chapter 40

🔲 Can I take the vow for Peace/non-violence? _____

🔲 Why or why not?

_____
_____
_____
_____
_____
_____
_____

## Chapter 41

Change takes place in _____.

Step one: _____.

Step two: _____.

When we release the old, we release old _____.

This old energy _____.

This serves two purposes:

1. _____
2. _____

◘ What disagreements do I currently have with another person?

_____
_____
_____
_____
_____
_____

## Chapter 42

### ELEMENT TWO – My Perspective Determines What I See

The past determines my _____.

My filter determines my _____.

My perspective is my _____.

When I change my _____, I change my _____.

All disagreements result from _____.

There are two possible perspectives: _____ or _____.

🔲 What previous life experiences filter the way I see life?

_____
_____
_____
_____
_____
_____

# Chapter 43

**ELEMENT THREE – I Always Get What I Desire**

Before birth, God programmed my spirit with my _____.

During childhood, society programs my body/ego to _____.

This produces a perspective of _____.

A perspective of duality causes _____.

However, I think conflict is caused by _____.

Change is _____.

Conflict is caused by a perspective of _____.

Conflict ends when I change my perspective to _____.

When my perspective is unity, everything leads to my _____.

**It is a Conspiracy for ME**

This quote changed Matt's perspective from duality to unity.

> *"It may seem like luck. It is not. The truth is that life is conspiring in your favor. It may not look that way at the time. However, everything that happens brings you closer to that which you Desire."*

◩ What does "Life is a Conspiracy for Me" mean to me?

_____
_____
_____

◩ Whom do I trust least?

_____

◩ What benefit do I receive from my relationship with this person?

_____
_____
_____

◩ How can I demonstrate love to this person?

_____
_____

## Chapter 44

Unity is _____.

I see others as _____.

A life of love and unity is a life without _____.

When I defend myself, I block _____.

No defense means no _____.

The most common barrier is _____.

Love is a process of _____.

Love is not _____.

Relationships function on _____.

Agreements are always made in the _____.

Marriage agreements enforce love by _____.

Unity means I _____.

If I perceive love as ownership, I experience _____ _____.

If I perceive love as unity, I experience _____ _____.

You and I are connected to one another. We are all connected to each other, to everything, and to God.

The reason we don't feel that connection is that we are defensive. We have barriers that hinder the connection.

However, when the defenses drop, when we become naked, when we truly love all without hesitancy, we experience the Law of Attraction without barriers.

When this takes place, you and I easily move towards our individual Desires.

In addition, we move towards our collective Desire, in perfect sync with one another, creating a world of beauty, awe, and majesty that ultimately brings us to World Peace.

▣ What causes me to feel naked/vulnerable?

_____

_____

_____

## Chapter 45

▣ Am I comfortable being physically naked with anyone in my life?

_____

▣ Who?

_____

▣ Would I be comfortable being physically naked with everyone in my life?

_____

▣ Why or why not?

_____

_____

- Am I comfortable being emotionally naked with anyone in my life?

  _____

- Who?

  _____

- Would I be comfortable being emotionally naked with everyone in my life?

  _____

- Why or why not?

  _____
  _____
  _____

# Chapter 46

- What current situation harms me the most?

  _____
  _____
  _____

- What benefit do I receive from this situation?

  _____
  _____
  _____
  _____

## Chapter 47

🌀 What agreement have I made in the past that I was not able to keep?

_____
_____
_____

🌀 Did the fear of loss prevent me from breaking the agreement?

_____

🌀 What agreement have I made with someone in the past that the other party was not able to keep?

_____
_____
_____
_____

🌀 Did the fear of loss prevent the other party from breaking the agreement?

_____

🌀 What agreements have I made in the past that I completely kept?

_____
_____
_____
_____
_____

🔲 Why are agreements so difficult to keep?

_____
_____
_____
_____
_____
_____

## Chapter 48

🔲 What defense mechanism can I drop today?

_____
_____

Steps to Relationship Peace of Mind:

Understand that like attracts like through _____
_____.

Develop a perspective of _____.

Drop all _____.

# Financial Peace of Mind

## Chapter 50

**The Law of Abundance -** _____
_____

- Do I feel like I live an abundant life?

_____

- Why or why not?

_____
_____
_____

## Chapter 51

- Do I live my life with an attitude of abundance or an attitude of lack?

_____
_____
_____
_____
_____

# Chapter 52

**The Three Elements of The Law of Abundance**

1. Abundance is a Normal Act of Nature
2. Lack is Always Temporary
3. Gratefulness Accelerates the Law of Abundance

**ELEMENT ONE: Abundance is a Normal Act of Nature**

Nature's design is reproduction through _____.

▫ What evidence of reproduction through multiplication do I see?

_____
_____
_____
_____

# Chapter 53

▫ What outside circumstances prevent my abundance?

_____
_____
_____
_____
_____

# Chapter 54

**ELEMENT TWO: Lack is Always Temporary**

▣ What does "Life is a Conspiracy for Me" mean to me?

_____

_____

_____

# Chapter 55

The only cause of lack is _____.

Preparation for abundance is always _____.

An example of Preparation for abundance is the _____.

If I see lack as anything else, I have a perspective of _____.

A perspective of duality causes _____, _____, and _____.

Fear, guilt, and blame sometimes feel like _____.

Guilt feels like _____ and gives me an excuse not to love myself so I can better love others.

Blame allows me to _____ because other people do the same thing so I think I am not so bad.

Fear feels like love because I'm _____ and others from outside dangers.

The evidence of fear, guilt, and blame is love with _____

Resistance creates _____.

🗗 What causes me to feel resistance?

_____
_____

🗗 Do I have hang-ups over money?

_____
_____

🗗 Am I struggling with how I'm going to pay bills?

_____
_____

🗗 Am I upset because the government is spending too much money?

_____
_____

## Chapter 56

Resistance causes me to see lack where there is _____.

🗗 What am I resistant to in my life today?

_____
_____
_____
_____

## Chapter 57

▣ What impossible situation do I face today?

_____
_____
_____
_____
_____
_____
_____

## Chapter 58

**ELEMENT THREE – Gratefulness Accelerates the Law of Abundance**

The best way to express gratefulness is through _____.

Generosity removes all _____.

▣ What thoughts do I have that resist abundance?

_____
_____
_____
_____
_____
_____
_____

## Chapter 59

Matt's observations regarding how to release resistance:

1. The Law of Attraction says I attract everything into my life.

2. If that is true, when I resist what arrives, it means I'm opposing the very thing I attracted.

3. This resistance creates an internal conflict.

4. I may recognize this conflict and release it through a religious experience or dream.

5. If I choose not to release the resistance, I may pass out, faint, become sick, or even end up in a coma in order for the resistance to disappear.

▢ Have I ever passed out?_____

▢ What happened? Describe it and identify lessons you learned.

_____
_____
_____
_____
_____
_____
_____
_____
_____
_____
_____
_____

# Chapter 60

🔲 Have I seen other people pass out? _____

🔲 What happened? Describe it and identify lessons you learned.

_____
_____
_____
_____
_____
_____
_____
_____
_____
_____
_____
_____
_____
_____
_____
_____
_____
_____
_____
_____
_____
_____
_____
_____
_____

# Chapter 61

- Have you experienced a life threatening accident? _____

- Write about it and identify the lessons you learned from it.

_____
_____
_____
_____
_____
_____
_____
_____
_____
_____
_____
_____
_____
_____
_____
_____
_____
_____
_____
_____

# Chapter 62

🔲 How do I release sickness?

_____

_____

🔲 Do I use traditional western medicine (surgery or medication) or another method?

_____

_____

🔲 Write about it.

_____

_____

_____

_____

_____

_____

_____

_____

_____

_____

_____

_____

_____

## Chapter 63

🌀 What pain and or sickness do I currently experience?

_____
_____


🌀 Do I use pain to prevent abundance? _____

🌀 How do I do this?

_____
_____
_____
_____
_____
_____
_____
_____
_____


## Chapter 64

🌀 How do I resist Love?

_____
_____
_____
_____
_____

## Chapter 65

▣ Have I ever experienced a dramatic release of resistance?_____

▣ List those experiences.

## Chapter 66

I respond in one of three ways when I receive something.

1. _____

2. _____

3. _____

When I share,

I _____.

When I keep,

I _____.

I _____.

◧ What clutters my life?

_____
_____
_____
_____
_____
_____
_____
_____
_____
_____
_____
_____

# Chapter 67

I cannot _____ at the same time.

When I resist something, I _____
_____.

What I resist _____.

When I share, I remove _____.

🔲 What possessions or people in my life distract me?

_____
_____
_____
_____
_____
_____

🔲 How can I immediately demonstrate gratefulness through an act of generosity?

_____
_____
_____
_____
_____
_____
_____

🔲 What can I share today?

_____
_____
_____
_____
_____
_____

## Chapter 68

Steps to Financial Peace of Mind:

Understand that abundance is _____.

Learn to release _____.

Practice acts of _____.

## NOTES

## What is the Next Step on My Journey to Peace of Mind?

The Peace of Mind philosophy taught in *Living the Southwest Lifestyle; How to Have and Maintain Peace of Mind* inspired the development of The Peace of Mind Training Institute, a tax-exempt organization. This training organization offers a variety of resources including workshops, webinars, coaching, books, audios, and videos. There is even an innovative Emissary Program if you decide a Peace of Mind career and business is right for you.

For most people, Peace of Mind Training Institute Workshops featured on the website are the next step. However, if you need individual assistance or have specific questions, we invite you to contact The Peace of Mind Training Institute directly for help in determining which step is right for you.

**Website:** www.PeaceofMindTrainingInstitute.com.
**Phone:** 505-286-5176
**Fax:** 505-286-1266
**Email:** Info@PeaceofMindTrainingInstitute.com
**Mailing Address:** 21 Pine Ridge Road, Sandia Park NM 87047

www.ingramcontent.com/pod-product-compliance
Lightning Source LLC
Chambersburg PA
CBHW081455060426
42444CB00037BA/3281